Making Money in 2024 and 2025 from Merch on Demand Sites

1. Introduction

1.1 Overview of Merch on Demand

Merch on demand (POD - Print on Demand) has rapidly become one of the most popular ways to make money online, especially for creatives and entrepreneurs looking to tap into the booming e-commerce market.

The concept is simple yet powerful: you create designs, upload them to a platform, and the platform handles production, shipping, and customer service.

When someone buys your design on a product like a t-shirt, mug, or phone case, you earn a royalty. The best part? You don't have to worry about inventory, upfront costs, or the logistics of selling physical products.

The popularity of merch on demand has grown exponentially over the past few years, driven by the desire for unique, personalized products and the ease of getting started.

Whether you're an artist looking to monetize your work, a social media influencer wanting to create branded merchandise, or an entrepreneur exploring new income streams, POD offers an accessible and scalable way to make money online.

1.2 Why 2024 and 2025 are Unique Opportunities

As we move into 2024 and 2025, the opportunities in the merch on demand market are more promising than ever before.

Several factors make these years unique and ripe for growth in the POD industry:

- Rise in E-commerce and Personalized Products:

E-commerce continues to grow globally, with more consumers turning to online shopping as their primary retail experience.

In particular, the demand for personalized and unique products is skyrocketing.

Consumers no longer want generic items; they seek products that reflect their personal style, interests, and values.

Merch on demand fulfills this need perfectly, allowing creators to offer a wide range of custom products.

- Technological Advancements:

 The technology behind POD platforms has advanced significantly, making it easier than ever to create and sell custom merchandise.

 From AI-powered design tools to advanced printing techniques, these innovations reduce barriers to entry, even for those with little to no design experience.

Additionally, improvements in data analytics help sellers better understand market trends and customer preferences, leading to more targeted and effective marketing strategies.

- Economic Factors:

 With economic uncertainty continuing in various parts of the world, many people are seeking alternative income streams.

 POD offers a low-risk way to generate additional revenue without significant upfront investment. Moreover, as the gig economy expands, more individuals are drawn to flexible, side-hustle opportunities that fit their lifestyles.

- Global Market Access:

 POD platforms are increasingly global, meaning your designs can reach customers all over the world.

 This broadens your potential customer base significantly, allowing for diverse and varied income streams depending on how well you can tap into different markets.

1.3 How to Use This Guide

This guide is designed for anyone looking to explore or expand their presence in the merch on demand industry.

Whether you're a complete beginner or someone with some experience looking to scale up, you'll find valuable insights and actionable advice here.

- Beginners will learn the fundamentals of setting up accounts, creating designs, and marketing their products.

- Intermediate sellers will gain advanced strategies for niche research, marketing, and scaling their business.

In the following sections, you'll discover a step-by-step approach to making money with merch on demand.

We'll cover everything from choosing the right platforms to using powerful tools, best practices for design, marketing strategies, and case studies of successful sellers.

This guide is packed with the tips and insights you need to thrive in 2024 and 2025.

2. Understanding the Merch on Demand Model

2.1 How Merch on Demand Works

Merch on demand operates on a simple yet effective model that allows creators to focus on what they do best—designing—while leaving the logistics of production, fulfillment, and customer service to the platform.

Here's how it works:

1. Create and Upload Designs:

As a seller, your primary task is to create unique designs that appeal to your target audience.

Once your designs are ready, you upload them to a POD platform like Amazon Merch, TeePublic, or Redbubble.

2. Choose Products to Sell:

After uploading your designs, you can choose which products you want to sell.

These can range from apparel like t-shirts and hoodies to accessories like phone cases, mugs, and tote bags.

Each platform offers different product options, so you can tailor your selections to what you think will sell best.

3. Set Pricing:

Most POD platforms allow you to set your own prices or choose from a range of pricing options.

The price you set will determine your profit margin, which is typically a percentage of the sale price after the platform takes its cut.

4. List Products for Sale:

Once your products are ready, they're listed on the platform's marketplace, where millions of potential customers can find and purchase them.

You can also promote your products through your own channels to drive traffic and increase sales.

5. Production and Fulfillment:

 When a customer orders one of your products, the POD platform takes care of everything from printing your design onto the product to packaging and shipping it directly to the customer.

 This is what makes POD so convenient—no inventory, no shipping logistics, and no upfront costs.

6. Earnings and Payouts:

After the platform deducts its fees, you earn a royalty on each sale.

Payouts typically occur on a monthly basis, although the frequency can vary depending on the platform.

2.2 Key Players in the Industry

The merch on demand industry is vast, with several key platforms dominating the market.

Each has its own unique features, strengths, and target audiences, making it important to choose the right one(s) for your business.

- Amazon Merch on Demand:

 Perhaps the most well-known and widely used POD platform, Amazon Merch offers unparalleled access to Amazon's massive customer base.
 It's particularly popular for apparel like t-shirts and hoodies. The platform is highly competitive, but it provides excellent potential for high-volume sales due to its sheer size and global reach. The application process can be selective, but once accepted, you gain access to powerful tools and analytics.

- TeePublic:

A favorite among artists and designers, TeePublic offers a wide range of products, from apparel to home decor. It's known for its vibrant community and focus on supporting independent artists.

TeePublic often promotes designs through its own marketing campaigns, giving sellers additional exposure. The platform also offers more control over pricing and product selection than some of its competitors.

- Redbubble:

Redbubble is another major player in the POD space, with a focus on high-quality art prints and unique designs. It's ideal for artists who want to showcase their work on a variety of products.

Redbubble is user-friendly and provides a supportive community for creators. Like TeePublic, it also markets products through its own channels, helping you reach a wider audience.

- Printful and Printify (Integrated Platforms):

 While not standalone marketplaces like the others, Printful and Printify allow you to integrate with e-commerce platforms like Shopify, Etsy, and WooCommerce.

 They handle production and fulfillment, giving you the flexibility to sell on multiple platforms and control your branding and customer experience.

2.3 Benefits and Challenges of Merch on Demand

Merch on demand offers numerous advantages, but it also comes with its own set of challenges.

Understanding these can help you navigate the industry more effectively.

Benefits:

- Low Upfront Costs:

 Unlike traditional retail, where you need to invest in inventory, POD requires no upfront investment.

 You only pay when a product is sold.

- Flexibility:

You can work from anywhere, create designs at your own pace, and scale your business as needed.

- Scalability:

Once you have a successful design, there's no limit to how much you can sell.

The platform handles all the logistics, allowing you to focus on creating more designs.

- Diverse Product Range:

 POD platforms offer a wide variety of products, enabling you to diversify your offerings and appeal to different market segments.

Challenges:

- High Competition:

 With low barriers to entry, the POD market is highly competitive.

 Standing out requires strong designs, effective marketing, and ongoing trend research.

- Platform Dependence:

 Your success is tied to the platform's rules and algorithms.

 Changes in policies or visibility algorithms can impact your sales.

- Lower Margins:

 Since the platform takes care of production and fulfillment, profit margins are typically lower compared to selling your own products directly. To earn significant income, you need to focus on volume.

- Marketing Effort Required:

 While some platforms do promote designs, you often need to invest time and resources into marketing your products to drive traffic and increase sales.

3. Getting Started with Merch on Demand

3.1 Initial Setup

The first step in your merch on demand journey is setting up accounts on the major platforms.

Here's how to get started:

Amazon Merch on Demand:

- Application Process:

Amazon Merch requires you to apply for an account. The application asks for basic information about your business and your experience with e-commerce.

Approval can take some time, and the process is selective, but it's worth the effort due to the platform's potential.

- Account Setup:

 Once approved, you can start setting up your account.

 This involves adding your payment details, tax information, and setting up your profile.

TeePublic:

- Sign-Up:

TeePublic has a straightforward sign-up process.

You can create an account quickly and start uploading designs almost immediately.

There's no application process, making it accessible to everyone.

- Profile Setup:

 Take time to fill out your profile, including adding a bio and linking your social media accounts.

 A well-completed profile can help attract customers and build credibility.

Redbubble:

- Creating an Account:

Similar to TeePublic, Redbubble has an easy sign-up process.

After creating your account, you can start uploading designs and setting up your store.

- Customizing Your Store:

 Redbubble allows for some customization of your storefront, including adding a banner, profile picture, and bio.

 Use these elements to create a professional and inviting store.

3.2 Researching Your Niche

Choosing the right niche is crucial to your success in the merch on demand industry.

A well-chosen niche allows you to stand out in a crowded market and attract a dedicated audience. Here's how to find the perfect niche:

- Use Google Trends:

 Google Trends is a powerful tool for identifying trending topics and niches.

 You can search for specific keywords to see how their popularity has changed over time and identify emerging trends.

- Merch Informer:

Merch Informer is a tool specifically designed for Amazon Merch sellers.

It helps you find profitable niches by analyzing sales data and competition.

You can search by keyword, category, or even specific design elements to find niches with high demand and low competition.

- Ahrefs:

Ahrefs is another excellent tool for niche research.

While it's primarily used for SEO, its keyword explorer feature can help you find popular keywords and content ideas that could inspire your designs.

Ahrefs also provides data on search volume and competition, helping you gauge the potential of different niches.

- Evaluate Competition:

 Once you've identified potential niches, it's important to evaluate the competition.

 Search for similar designs on the platform you're using and see how they're performing.

 Look for gaps in the market where you can offer something unique or better.

- Understand Your Audience:

 Knowing who you're designing for is key.

 Consider demographics like age, gender, interests, and buying behavior.

 The better you understand your target audience, the more effectively you can create designs that resonate with them.

3.3 Designing for Success

Your designs are the heart of your merch on demand business.

The quality, originality, and appeal of your designs will determine your success.

Here are some tips to help you create winning designs:

- Eye-Catching Designs:

 Your designs need to grab attention.

 Focus on bold colors, clear typography, and strong visuals.

 Simplicity often works best, especially on products like t-shirts and hoodies.

Design Tools:

Whether you're a seasoned designer or a beginner, there are tools to help you create professional-quality designs:

- Adobe Illustrator:

The industry standard for vector design, Illustrator is perfect for creating scalable, high-quality graphics.

- Canva:

 Canva is a user-friendly tool ideal for beginners.

 It offers a range of templates and design elements that make it easy to create professional designs quickly.

- Affinity Designer:

 A more affordable alternative to Illustrator, Affinity Designer offers robust vector design capabilities.

Originality:

Avoid copying popular designs. Not only is this unethical, but it also limits your potential for success.

Focus on creating original designs that reflect your unique style or niche.

Originality is key to building a brand and attracting loyal customers.

Design Quality:

High-resolution designs are essential for POD.

Ensure your files are large enough to print clearly on all products, and double-check for any issues (like misspellings) before uploading.

3.4 Uploading Your Designs

Once your designs are ready, it's time to upload them to your chosen platform.

Here's a step-by-step guide:

- File Formats and Requirements:
Each platform has specific file format requirements. Typically, you'll need to upload high-resolution PNG files with a transparent background. Make sure to check each platform's guidelines for dimensions and file size.

- Product Selection:

After uploading your design, you'll need to choose which products to offer.

Select a range of products that best showcase your design.

Some designs may work better on certain products, so be selective.

- Optimizing Titles and Descriptions:

 Your product title and description are crucial for SEO and attracting customers.

 Use relevant keywords that potential buyers might search for.

 Make sure your titles are clear and descriptive, and include key details in the description to help with visibility.

- Tags and Keywords:

  Most platforms allow you to add tags or keywords to help categorize your product.

  Use all available slots with relevant keywords to increase the chances of your products being found.

- Preview and Final Check:

 Before publishing, use the platform's preview tool to see how your design looks on each product.

 Make any necessary adjustments and ensure everything looks perfect.

4. Tools and Resources for Merch Success

4.1 Design Tools and Software

Creating high-quality designs is essential for success in the merch on demand business.

Fortunately, there are numerous tools available to help you design like a pro, regardless of your skill level.

Free Design Tools:

- GIMP:

GIMP is a free and open-source alternative to Photoshop. It offers a wide range of features for creating and editing designs.

While it has a steeper learning curve than some other tools, it's a powerful option for those on a budget.

- Inkscape:

 Inkscape is another free tool, specifically for vector graphics.

 It's a great alternative to Adobe Illustrator and is perfect for creating scalable designs that can be used across various products.

- Krita:

Krita is a free, open-source painting program that's excellent for artists who prefer a more traditional drawing experience.

It's ideal for creating unique, hand-drawn designs.

Paid Design Tools:

- Adobe Illustrator:
 As mentioned earlier, Illustrator is the industry standard for vector design.
 It offers extensive features and precision for creating detailed, professional-quality designs.

- Photoshop:
 Photoshop is another staple for designers, particularly for editing images and creating complex graphics. It's versatile and widely used across various creative industries.

- Affinity Designer:

 Affinity Designer is a powerful, cost-effective alternative to Illustrator, offering many of the same features at a fraction of the cost.

- Procreate:

 For those who prefer designing on a tablet, Procreate is a popular app for the iPad. It's user-friendly and excellent for creating hand-drawn designs.

Plugins and Resources for Design Enhancement:

- Creative Market:

A marketplace for design assets like fonts, graphics, and templates.

It's a valuable resource for enhancing your designs.

- Envato Elements:

A subscription service offering a vast library of design resources, including templates, fonts, and graphics.

It's an excellent investment for designers looking to expand their toolkit.

- Adobe Stock:

Adobe's stock library offers millions of images, illustrations, and vectors that you can incorporate into your designs.

It's particularly useful for finding high-quality assets to complement your work.

4.2 Keyword and Trend Research Tools

Understanding what customers are searching for is key to creating designs that sell.

The following tools can help you identify trending keywords, popular niches, and high-demand products.

Merch Informer:

- Specifically designed for Amazon Merch sellers, Merch Informer provides keyword research, trend analysis, and niche validation tools.

It's an invaluable resource for finding profitable niches and understanding what's currently in demand on Amazon.

Jungle Scout:

- Jungle Scout is a comprehensive tool for Amazon sellers, offering insights into product trends, keyword research, and competitive analysis.

While it's primarily used for FBA (Fulfillment by Amazon) sellers, it's also useful for POD sellers on Amazon Merch.

Helium 10:

- Helium 10 is another powerful tool for Amazon sellers, offering a suite of features for keyword research, listing optimization, and product tracking.

It's particularly useful for identifying high-traffic keywords and optimizing your product listings.

Google Trends:

- Google Trends is a free tool that shows how search terms are trending over time.

It's useful for identifying emerging trends and seasonal spikes in interest, allowing you to create designs that capitalize on these trends.

Pinterest Trends:

- Pinterest Trends helps you see what's popular on Pinterest, which is often a good indicator of broader consumer trends.

It's especially useful for visual inspiration and identifying trending aesthetics.

4.3 Analytics and Monitoring Tools

To grow your POD business, it's essential to track your performance and make data-driven decisions.

Here are some tools to help you monitor your sales, analyze customer behavior, and optimize your strategies.

Google Analytics:

- Google Analytics is a must-have tool for tracking website traffic, user behavior, and conversion rates.

 If you have your own e-commerce site or drive traffic from social media to your POD store, Google Analytics provides valuable insights into what's working and where you can improve.

Amazon Brand Analytics:

- For Amazon Merch sellers, Amazon Brand Analytics offers detailed data on customer search behavior, competitor analysis, and market trends.

 This information can help you refine your product offerings and marketing strategies.

Redbubble Dashboard:

- Redbubble provides a built-in dashboard that tracks your sales, views, and engagement metrics.

It's a handy tool for monitoring your performance on the platform and identifying your best-selling products.

TeePublic Analytics:

- TeePublic also offers analytics tools to help you understand your sales performance, including data on earnings, traffic sources, and customer demographics.

 Use this information to optimize your store and target your marketing efforts more effectively.

4.4 Social Media and Marketing Tools

Marketing is crucial for driving traffic to your POD store and increasing sales.

Here are some tools to help you manage and optimize your social media and marketing efforts.

Buffer and Hootsuite:

- Both Buffer and Hootsuite are social media management tools that allow you to schedule posts, track engagement, and manage multiple social media accounts from one dashboard.

These tools save time and help you maintain a consistent social media presence.

Canva and Adobe Spark:

- Canva and Adobe Spark are excellent tools for creating social media graphics, promotional banners, and marketing materials.

 They offer easy-to-use templates that help you create professional-looking content quickly.

Tailwind:

- Tailwind is a scheduling tool specifically for Pinterest and Instagram.

It's particularly useful for planning and automating your Pinterest marketing, which can be a powerful traffic driver for POD products.

Facebook Ads Manager:

- If you're running paid ads on Facebook or Instagram, Facebook Ads Manager is the tool you'll use to create, manage, and optimize your campaigns.

It offers detailed targeting options, allowing you to reach your ideal audience with precision.

5. Marketing and Promoting Your Merchandise

5.1 Understanding the Importance of Marketing

While creating great designs is crucial, marketing is the engine that drives sales in the merch on demand business.

Even the best designs won't sell if no one sees them, so it's essential to invest time and effort into promoting your products.

Effective marketing helps you reach a broader audience, build brand recognition, and ultimately increase your sales.

There are two primary marketing strategies: organic and paid. Organic marketing involves free methods like social media posts, SEO, and content creation, while paid marketing includes ads on platforms like Facebook, Instagram, and Google. Both strategies have their place in a successful POD business, and a combination of the two is often the most effective approach.

5.2 Social Media Marketing

Social media is one of the most powerful tools for promoting your POD products.

Platforms like Instagram, Pinterest, TikTok, and Facebook allow you to showcase your designs, connect with your audience, and drive traffic to your store.

Here's how to leverage each platform effectively:

Instagram:

- Visual Appeal:

 Instagram is a highly visual platform, making it perfect for showcasing your designs.

 Post high-quality images of your products, lifestyle shots, and behind-the-scenes content to engage your audience.

- Hashtags:

 Use relevant hashtags to increase the visibility of your posts.

 Research popular hashtags in your niche and include a mix of broad and specific tags to reach a wider audience.

- Stories and Reels:

 Instagram Stories and Reels are great for sharing quick, engaging content.

 Use them to announce new designs, share promotions, or give followers a glimpse into your creative process.

- Engagement:

Engage with your audience by responding to comments, liking their posts, and using polls or Q&A features in Stories to build community.

Pinterest:

- Pin Consistently:

 Pinterest is a powerful platform for driving traffic, especially for niche products.

 Create visually appealing pins and post consistently to keep your content fresh and discoverable.

- Use Keywords:

 Optimize your pin descriptions with relevant keywords to improve your chances of appearing in search results.

 Focus on terms that your target audience might search for when looking for products like yours.

- Group Boards:

 Join group boards in your niche to increase the reach of your pins.

 Contributing to active boards can help you tap into a larger audience.

- Promoted Pins:

 Consider using Promoted Pins to boost visibility.

 Pinterest ads are relatively inexpensive and can drive significant traffic to your store if targeted correctly.

TikTok:

- Short, Engaging Videos:

TikTok's short-form video format is perfect for quick product showcases, tutorials, or creative content that features your designs.

Focus on creating fun, engaging videos that capture attention quickly.

- Trends and Challenges:

  Participate in TikTok trends and challenges to increase your visibility.

  Using trending sounds or hashtags can help your content go viral.

- Influencer Collaborations:

  Partner with TikTok influencers who align with your brand to reach new audiences.

  Influencer marketing on TikTok can be highly effective, especially for niche products.

Facebook:

- Business Page:

 Set up a Facebook Business Page for your store.

 This serves as a hub where you can post updates, share new designs, and engage with your audience.

- Groups:

 Join and participate in relevant Facebook Groups where your target audience hangs out.

 Engage in discussions and share your products when appropriate to build awareness.

- Facebook Shops:

 Consider setting up a Facebook Shop where users can browse and purchase your products directly on the platform.

 This can streamline the buying process and increase sales.

5.3 Influencer and Affiliate Marketing

Influencer and affiliate marketing can be powerful tools for expanding your reach and boosting sales.

These strategies involve partnering with individuals who have a strong following and can promote your products to their audience.

Influencer Marketing:

- Finding Influencers:

 Look for influencers who align with your brand and have an engaged following in your niche.

 Micro-influencers (those with smaller, highly engaged audiences) can often be more effective and affordable than bigger names.

- Collaboration Ideas:

 Work with influencers to create sponsored posts, product reviews, or giveaways.

 These collaborations can introduce your products to new audiences and drive sales.

- Tracking Results:

 Use tracking links or discount codes to measure the effectiveness of your influencer campaigns.

 This data will help you determine which collaborations are worth continuing.

Affiliate Marketing:

- Setting Up an Affiliate Program:

 Platforms like Amazon and Redbubble offer built-in affiliate programs, or you can create your own using tools like ShareASale or Refersion.

 Affiliates promote your products and earn a commission on each sale they generate.

- Recruiting Affiliates:

 Reach out to bloggers, social media influencers, and websites that align with your brand to join your affiliate program.

 Offer competitive commissions and promotional materials to encourage them to promote your products.

- Monitoring Performance:

 Track your affiliates' performance through your affiliate platform.

 Regularly review their sales and provide them with support and incentives to keep them motivated.

5.4 Paid Advertising

Paid advertising can be a highly effective way to drive traffic and sales, especially when combined with organic marketing efforts.

Here's how to get started with paid ads:

Facebook and Instagram Ads:

- Targeting:

 Facebook's ad platform offers robust targeting options, allowing you to reach your ideal customers based on demographics, interests, and behaviors.

 Use lookalike audiences to target users similar to your existing customers.

- Ad Formats:

 Experiment with different ad formats, including carousel ads, video ads, and dynamic product ads.

 Test which formats perform best for your products.

- Budgeting:

 Start with a small budget to test different ads and audiences.

 As you gather data, optimize your campaigns and scale up your budget for the best-performing ads.

Google Ads:

- Search Ads:

Google Search Ads can help you capture intent-driven traffic by targeting users who are actively searching for products like yours.

Use relevant keywords and compelling ad copy to attract clicks.

- Shopping Ads:

Google Shopping Ads display your products directly in search results, complete with images, prices, and reviews.

These ads are highly effective for e-commerce, as they allow users to see your products at a glance.

- Display Ads:

 Google Display Ads can help you reach users across the web by showing your ads on websites and apps that are part of Google's network.

 Use eye-catching visuals and clear calls to action to drive traffic.

Pinterest Ads:

- Promoted Pins:

 Promoted Pins are a great way to increase the visibility of your products on Pinterest.

 Target your ads based on keywords, interests, and demographics to reach the right audience.

- Video Ads:

 Pinterest Video Ads are highly engaging and can help you showcase your products in action.

 Use short, attention-grabbing videos to tell a story or demonstrate the value of your products.

TikTok Ads:

- In-Feed Ads:

 TikTok's In-Feed Ads appear in users' feeds as they scroll through content.

 These ads blend seamlessly with organic content, making them less intrusive and more engaging.

- Branded Hashtag Challenges:

 Create a branded hashtag challenge to encourage user-generated content and increase brand awareness.

 This type of campaign can quickly go viral if done right.

Monitoring and Optimization:

- Track Performance:

 Use the analytics tools provided by each ad platform to monitor your campaign performance.

 Track key metrics like click-through rate (CTR), conversion rate, and return on ad spend (ROAS).

- A/B Testing:

 Continuously test different ad creatives, targeting options, and bidding strategies to find what works best.

 A/B testing helps you optimize your campaigns for better results.

- Scaling Successful Campaigns:

 Once you identify successful campaigns, scale them up by increasing your budget or expanding your target audience.

 Keep testing and optimizing to maintain performance as you scale.

6. Best Practices for Long-Term Success

6.1 Consistent Quality and Brand Building

Consistency is key to building a successful merch on demand business.

Maintaining high design quality and delivering a consistent brand experience will help you build trust with your customers and encourage repeat purchases.

Design Quality:

- Maintain High Standards:

Always prioritize quality over quantity.

It's better to have a few well-designed products than a large catalog of mediocre items.

- Customer Feedback:

 Pay attention to customer reviews and feedback.

 If customers consistently praise certain aspects of your designs or products, make those elements a staple of your brand.

- Stay Updated:

 Keep your design skills sharp by staying updated with the latest trends and techniques.

 Regularly update your portfolio with fresh designs to keep your store appealing.

Brand Building:

- Develop a Unique Style:

Your brand should have a distinct and recognizable style.

Whether it's through color schemes, typography, or design themes, consistency in your branding helps create a memorable identity.

- Create a Brand Story:

  Share your brand's story with your audience.

  Explain the inspiration behind your designs, your creative process, or the values that drive your business.

  A compelling brand story can foster a deeper connection with your customers.

- Build Customer Loyalty:

 Offer incentives for repeat customers, such as discounts, exclusive designs, or early access to new products.

 Loyal customers are more likely to recommend your brand to others.

6.2 Keeping Up with Trends

Staying on top of trends is crucial for keeping your designs relevant and appealing to your target audience.

Here's how to stay updated:

Trend Research:

- Regularly Use Research Tools:

  Continuously monitor tools like Google Trends, Pinterest Trends, and Merch Informer to stay ahead of emerging trends.

  Set up alerts for specific keywords or categories to receive updates as trends evolve.

- Follow Industry Influencers:

 Keep an eye on influencers, bloggers, and thought leaders in your niche.

 They often have their fingers on the pulse of what's trending and can provide valuable insights into what's popular.

- Seasonal Trends:

 Plan your designs around seasonal trends and events.

 Holidays, sports seasons, and cultural events often drive significant spikes in demand for themed merchandise.

Adapting to Trends:

- Be Agile:

 The ability to quickly adapt to trends can give you a competitive edge.

 When you spot a trend gaining traction, move quickly to create and launch relevant designs.

- Balance Trends with Timelessness:

While it's important to capitalize on trends, don't lose sight of timeless designs that can generate steady sales over time.

A balanced approach helps ensure long-term success.

6.3 Scaling Your Business

As your POD business grows, you'll need to scale your operations to keep up with demand and maximize your profits.

Here are some strategies to help you scale effectively:

Expanding Your Product Line:

- Diversify Product Offerings:

 Consider expanding your product range to include more items, such as accessories, home decor, or seasonal products.

 Offering a variety of products increases your chances of appealing to a broader audience.

- Test New Niches:

Once you've established a successful niche, explore adjacent or complementary niches.

This diversification can help you reach new customer segments and reduce your reliance on a single niche.

Outsourcing Design Work:

- Hire Freelance Designers:

As your business grows, consider hiring freelance designers to help you create more designs.

Platforms like Upwork and Fiverr are great places to find talented designers.

- Design Collaboration:

Collaborate with other designers or artists to create unique, co-branded products.

These collaborations can bring fresh perspectives and expand your audience.

Streamlining Operations:

- Automate Repetitive Tasks:

 Use tools and software to automate tasks like social media posting, customer communication, and inventory management.

 Automation frees up your time to focus on more strategic aspects of your business.

- Use Fulfillment Services:

 If you're selling through your own website, consider using fulfillment services like Printful or Printify to handle production and shipping.

 This allows you to scale without worrying about logistics.

Building a Team:

- Hire Virtual Assistants:

As your workload increases, hiring a virtual assistant can help you manage tasks like customer service, order processing, and social media management.

- Develop a Support Network:

 Join POD communities and networks where you can exchange ideas, seek advice, and collaborate with other sellers.

 Building a support network can provide valuable insights and help you navigate the challenges of scaling.

7. Case Studies: Successful Merch on Demand Sellers

7.1 Success Stories from Amazon Merch

Hypothetical Case Study 1: The Power of Niche Targeting

- Background:

 A seller focusing on a specific hobby niche, such as gardening or vintage cars, identified a gap in the market where demand was high but competition was low.

- Strategy:

 By creating high-quality designs tailored to the interests of this niche audience, the seller quickly gained traction.

 They used tools like Merch Informer to identify popular keywords and focused on producing designs that resonated with their target market.

- Outcome:

The seller built a loyal customer base and achieved consistent monthly sales, with some designs becoming evergreen products that continued to sell year-round.

Hypothetical Case Study 2: Seasonal Success with Trendspotting

- Background:
 Another seller capitalized on seasonal trends, particularly around major holidays like Christmas and Halloween.

- Strategy:
 They used Google Trends and social media insights to predict which themes and designs would be popular each season. By preparing designs months in advance, they were ready to launch when demand spiked.

- Outcome:

The seller experienced significant sales during holiday seasons, with some products achieving bestseller status on Amazon Merch.

This seasonal strategy provided a substantial income boost each year.

7.2 TeePublic and Redbubble Success

Hypothetical Case Study 3: Building a Brand on TeePublic

- Background:

A graphic designer decided to turn their passion for retro and vintage-inspired designs into a brand on TeePublic.

- Strategy:

The designer focused on creating a cohesive brand aesthetic that appealed to a specific audience interested in nostalgia and retro culture.

They consistently uploaded new designs and engaged with their audience on social media, driving traffic to their TeePublic store.

- Outcome:

Over time, the designer built a strong brand presence on TeePublic, leading to a steady stream of sales and loyal customers.

Their store became known for its unique style, and they expanded into collaborations and custom design requests.

Hypothetical Case Study 4: Redbubble Artist's Journey to Success

- Background:

An artist with a distinct illustration style started uploading their work to Redbubble without much expectation.

However, they soon realized the potential of the platform.

- Strategy:

 The artist focused on creating unique, high-quality illustrations that stood out in the crowded marketplace.

 They also leveraged social media, particularly Instagram and Pinterest, to showcase their work and drive traffic to their Redbubble store.

- Outcome:

 The artist's consistent effort paid off, with their designs being featured on Redbubble's homepage and in various collections.

 This exposure led to increased sales, and they eventually became one of the top sellers on the platform.

7.3 Lessons Learned from These Hypothetical Case Studies

- Niche Targeting is Powerful: Finding and focusing on a specific niche can help you stand out in a crowded market and build a loyal customer base.

- Seasonal Trends Can Boost Sales: Capitalizing on seasonal trends and holidays can lead to significant sales spikes, especially if you plan and launch your designs at the right time.

- Brand Consistency Matters: Building a consistent brand identity helps attract and retain customers. Whether it's through a distinct design style or a cohesive theme, consistency is key to long-term success.

- Leverage Multiple Channels: Successful sellers often use a combination of platforms and marketing channels to reach a wider audience and increase sales.

8. Common Mistakes to Avoid

8.1 Not Doing Proper Research

One of the biggest mistakes POD sellers make is not doing enough research before launching their products.

Without proper research, you risk entering a saturated market, targeting the wrong audience, or creating designs that don't resonate with potential buyers.

Research Tips:

- Use tools like Google Trends, Merch Informer, and Ahrefs to identify profitable niches and keywords.

- Analyze the competition to see what's already available and identify gaps in the market.

- Understand your target audience's preferences and behaviors before creating your designs.

8.2 Poor Quality Designs

Low-quality designs can severely impact your sales and reputation.

Customers are more likely to purchase products with clear, well-executed designs that reflect a professional level of quality.

Quality Tips:

- Invest time in learning design principles or hire a professional designer if needed.

- Use high-resolution files and ensure your designs meet the platform's technical requirements.

- Avoid overly complex designs that might not translate well onto different products.

8.3 Ignoring Marketing

Many sellers mistakenly believe that simply uploading their designs will lead to sales.

However, without marketing, your products may never be seen by potential customers.

Marketing Tips:

- Develop a marketing strategy that includes social media, influencer partnerships, and paid advertising.

- Engage with your audience regularly and build a community around your brand.

- Use SEO and keyword optimization to improve your product visibility on the platform.

8.4 Not Diversifying Your Product Line

Focusing too narrowly on a single product type or niche can limit your growth potential.

Diversifying your product offerings can help you reach a broader audience and increase your chances of success.

Diversification Tips:

- Experiment with different product types, such as apparel, accessories, and home decor.

- Explore new niches or themes that complement your existing designs.

- Regularly update your store with fresh designs to keep it appealing to returning customers.

9. Future Trends in Merch on Demand

9.1 Emerging Technologies

The merch on demand industry is constantly evolving, with new technologies shaping the future of design, production, and marketing.

AI and Machine Learning:

- AI is increasingly being used to automate design processes, from generating design ideas to optimizing product listings.

Machine learning algorithms can also help sellers predict trends and personalize marketing efforts.

Augmented Reality (AR):

- AR technology is starting to be used in e-commerce to allow customers to visualize products in their own environment before purchasing.

This trend could become more prominent in the POD industry, enhancing the online shopping experience and reducing return rates.

9.2 Environmental and Ethical Considerations

As consumers become more conscious of environmental and ethical issues, sustainability is becoming a key trend in the POD industry.

Sustainable Materials:

- More POD platforms are starting to offer eco-friendly products made from sustainable materials.

Choosing to sell these products can help you appeal to environmentally conscious consumers and differentiate your brand.

Ethical Production:

- Transparency in production practices is increasingly important to customers.

 Highlighting the ethical aspects of your products, such as fair labor practices and eco-friendly printing methods, can build trust with your audience.

9.3 New Platforms and Marketplaces

While Amazon Merch, TeePublic, and Redbubble remain dominant, new platforms and marketplaces are emerging, offering fresh opportunities for sellers.

Emerging Platforms:

- Keep an eye on new POD platforms that cater to specific niches or offer unique selling features.

Joining a new platform early can give you a competitive advantage.

- Consider marketplaces that focus on handmade, customized, or artisanal products, as these often attract a different audience than traditional POD platforms.

9.4 Predictions for 2024 and 2025

The future of merch on demand looks promising, with continued growth driven by technological advancements, shifting consumer preferences, and the expansion of e-commerce.

Continued Growth in Personalized Products:

- The demand for personalized products will likely continue to rise, with consumers seeking items that reflect their individual tastes and values.

Sellers who can offer unique, customizable designs will be well-positioned for success.

Increased Focus on Sustainability:

- Sustainability will become increasingly important, with more consumers seeking eco-friendly products.

 Sellers who prioritize sustainability in their designs and product offerings will stand out in the market.

Expansion into New Markets:

- As e-commerce continues to grow globally, there will be opportunities to reach new markets, particularly in emerging economies.

Sellers who can adapt their offerings to different cultures and preferences will benefit from this expansion.

10. Conclusion

10.1 Recap of Key Points

Making money through merch on demand in 2024 and 2025 offers incredible opportunities, especially with the right strategies and tools.

By choosing the right platforms, conducting thorough research, creating high-quality designs, and effectively marketing your products, you can build a successful POD business.

- Niche Research:

 Identify profitable niches with low competition and high demand.

- Quality Designs:

 Focus on creating original, high-quality designs that resonate with your target audience.

- Effective Marketing:

 Invest time in both organic and paid marketing strategies to drive traffic and increase sales.

- Consistency and Scaling:

 Maintain consistent quality, keep up with trends, and scale your business by diversifying your product line and outsourcing tasks as needed.

10.2 Encouragement to Start Your Journey

Starting a merch on demand business can be both exciting and rewarding.

With low upfront costs, flexible working conditions, and the potential for significant income, it's an opportunity worth exploring. Don't be discouraged by challenges or competition—every successful seller started somewhere, and with dedication and creativity, you can carve out your own success in this thriving industry.

10.3 Final Tips and Resources

As you embark on your merch on demand journey, here are a few final tips to keep in mind:

- Stay Persistent:

Success in POD doesn't happen overnight. Be patient, keep refining your designs, and stay committed to your goals.

- Learn Continuously:

The POD industry is constantly evolving. Keep learning about new tools, trends, and strategies to stay ahead of the competition.

- Connect with the Community:

Join online communities, forums, and social media groups related to POD. Connecting with other sellers can provide valuable insights, support, and collaboration opportunities.

Additional Resources:

- Books:
 "Crushing It!" by Gary Vaynerchuk, "The Lean Startup" by Eric Ries.

- Online Courses:
 Udemy and Skillshare offer courses on POD, digital marketing, and graphic design.

- Podcasts:
 "Side Hustle School," "Print on Demand Cast," "The EcomCrew Podcast."

Please use the next few pages for your notes and debates.

www.ingramcontent.com/pod-product-compliance
Lightning Source LLC
Chambersburg PA
CBHW052154220526
45471CB00004B/1677